People Are Starting to Complain

People Are Starting to Complain

A COLLECTION OF SUNDAY COMICS
BY JIM UNGER

Andrews, McMeel & Parker
A Universal Press Syndicate Company
Kansas City • New York

ISBN: 0-8362-2058-7

Library of Congress Catalog Card Number: 84-81549

5

6

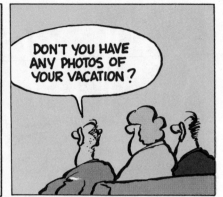

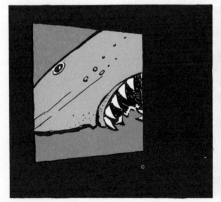

14

15

HERMAN

by JIM UNGER

MY FAMILY ALWAYS WAS POLITICAL.

MY SISTER'S ON A HUNGER STRIKE TO PROTEST THE ARMS RACE.

...AND GUESS WHO'S GOING TO ADDRESS THE GENERAL ASSEMBLY OF THE UNITED NATIONS IN A PLEA FOR SANITY...

GUESS...

PROBABLY THE MANAGER OF HER LOCAL SUPERMARKET.

HERMAN by JIM UNGER

NO MORE WASHDAY BLUES...

WHEN MY HUSBAND COMES HOME FROM WORK, HE'S COVERED IN GREASE.

GREASE AND DIRT ON HIS SHIRT...ON HIS PANTS...IN HIS SOCKS...AND YES, EVEN ON HIS UNDERWEAR...

LUCKILY, I NOW HAVE THE ALL-NEW, POWERFUL.....

...'WHACKO.'

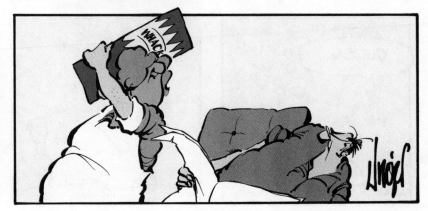

27

29

31

HERMAN by JIM UNGER

WHAT A LIFE!

HIGH SCHOOL DIPLOMA...AND I'VE BEEN OUT OF WORK FOR TWO YEARS.

THERE'S A GUY HERE, STARTED WASHING DISHES AND MADE TEN MILLION BUCKS WITH A CHAIN OF RESTAURANTS.

...WITH A GRADE THREE EDUCATION!

THAT COULD BE YOUR PROBLEM, RIGHT THERE.

YOU'RE OVERQUALIFIED...

34

37

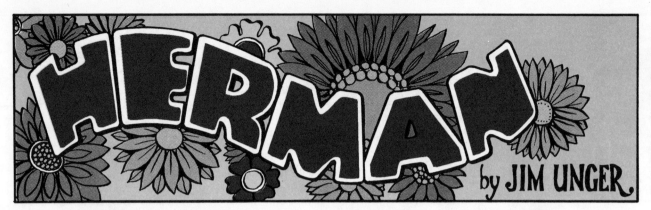

...ER... EXCUSE ME...

YOU'VE BEEN HERE FOR QUITE A WHILE NOW... DO YOU NEED HELP?

SIXTY YEARS AGO, CROSSING THIS STREET WAS A PIECE OF CAKE.... NOW, EVERYBODY THINKS IT'S A RACETRACK!!!

BUT THERE HASN'T BEEN A CAR FOR AT LEAST TEN MINUTES!

I NEED LONGER THAN THAT!

"HERE, YOU'RE ALWAYS SAYING WOMEN ARE BETTER THAN MEN... TRY CUTTING SOME WOOD TO BUILD A FIRE..."

I CAN'T BELIEVE WE HAVEN'T SEEN EACH OTHER FOR 30 YEARS!

40

HERMAN by JIM UNGER

STRIKE

WHAT'S BEHIND THIS STRIKE?

THERE HAS BEEN A BREAKDOWN IN THE DIALOGUE WITH REGARD TO THE INDEXING OF R.V.U.W. BENEFITS WITH PROVISIONAL MODIFICATIONS.

BASICALLY.... THEY DO NOT PERTAIN TO SICK LEAVE OR OVERTIME.. ..AND UNTIL THE W.W.P.W. IS RECOGNIZED BY THE EMPLOYERS, AS WAS PREVIOUSLY AGREED UPON, WE SHALL BE COMPELLED TO INVOKE 'SECTION FOUR' IN THE BEST INTERESTS OF A DEMOCRATIC RESOLUTION.

FURTHERMORE...THE L.O.S.B., HISTORICALLY APPLICABLE IN THIS INSTANCE, SHOULD NOT BE OVERLOOKED IN THE NEGOTIATIONS WHICH ARE CURRENTLY IN PROGRESS.

WHAT DOES ALL THAT MEAN?

..ABOUT SEVEN BUCKS A WEEK.

I HAVE SOME GOOD NEWS FOR YOU, SMITH.

I ADVISED THE BOARD MEMBERS THAT YOU FIND IT IMPOSSIBLE TO CONTINUE WITH US AT YOUR PRESENT SALARY....

..AND THEY AGREED WITH ME THAT IN VIEW OF YOUR ELEVEN YEARS OF LOYALTY TO THIS COMPANY...

...THERE IS MORE INVOLVED HERE THAN MERE MONEY.

EVEN IN THESE DIFFICULT AND TROUBLED TIMES..

.. A FEW EXTRA DOLLARS WON'T SINK THE SHIP.

WE'VE DECIDED TO GIVE YOU A "GOING AWAY PARTY."

47

51

54

HERMAN

by JIM UNGER

NOW LET ME SEE IF I HAVE THE FACTS STRAIGHT.

MR. BREWSTER... YOU SAY YOU'RE 95 YEARS OLD.

HE'S 97.

SHE'S NOT 92, SHE'S 93.

YOU'VE BEEN MARRIED FOR 76 YEARS... YOU HAVE 14 CHILDREN, 37 GRANDCHILDREN AND 68 GREAT-GRANDCHILDREN.

THAT'S ABOUT RIGHT.

...NOW YOU BOTH WANT A DIVORCE.

CORRECT.

ON WHAT GROUNDS?

INCOMPATIBILITY.

HERMAN
by JIM UNGER

SOMEONE'S WAVING!

GREETINGS FROM THE KING OF....

NAME?

CHRIS.....ER.. COLUMBUS...C.

I AM A REPRESENTATIVE OF HIS MAJESTY...

IT SAYS HERE YOU ARE A SELF-EMPLOYED NAVIGATOR... WHAT'S THE PURPOSE OF YOUR VISIT?

VACATION.

ANY ALCOHOL?... FIREARMS?...GIFTS? ARE YOU CARRYING MORE THAN 500 COCONUTS?

NOPE.

OVER THERE.

NEXT.

HERMAN

by JIM UNGER

HOW D'YOU FEEL?

SEE THAT WOMAN IN THE NEXT BED? HER HUSBAND BRINGS HER FRESH FLOWERS EVERY DAY.

HE SAID HER SURROUNDINGS SHOULD ALWAYS BE BEAUTIFUL.

HE'S A WIMP.

IN THIRTY YEARS, WHEN HAVE YOU EVER TRIED TO MAKE MY SURROUNDINGS MORE BEAUTIFUL?

NOT ONCE.

WHAT ABOUT WHEN I THREW OUT ALL THOSE PICTURES OF YOUR MOTHER?

58

THANK YOU FOR COMING.

GENTLEMEN... BY CONVERTING SPEECH INTO ELECTRICAL IMPULSES, I CAN SEND IT ALONG A WIRE AND CONVERSE WITH SOMEONE IN THE NEXT ROOM OR MILES AWAY.

IN A FEW MINUTES, I WILL DEMONSTRATE MY NEW TELEPHONIC DEVICE RIGHT HERE BEFORE YOUR EYES AND YOUR EARS....

PREPARE YOURSELVES, GENTLEMEN, FOR THE TWENTIETH CENTURY.

DING DONG

HE'S EARLY.

HERE WE GO...

ONE SMALL STEP FOR MAN..

.........IS THAT CITY MEAT MARKET?

IT'S QUITE SIMPLE.

A CHOCOLATE CAKE COMES ALONG HERE EVERY ONE AND A HALF SECONDS...

YOU HAVE TO ARRANGE FIVE CHERRIES ON EACH CAKE.

IF YOU THINK YOU CAN HANDLE IT, YOU CAN HAVE THE JOB... FOR A TRIAL PERIOD.

WHAT'S THE TRIAL PERIOD?

FIFTEEN SECONDS.

HERMAN
by JIM UNGER

WHAT'S IN THE PARCEL?

YOU KNOW THAT CORRESPONDENCE COURSE I'VE BEEN TAKING ON SELF-DEFENSE?

WHAT ABOUT IT?

THIS... IS THE FINAL EXAMINATION.

YOU'VE BEEN DOING IT FOR FIVE YEARS!

THIS IS ALL THAT STANDS BETWEEN ME AND MY DIPLOMA...

68

YOU BACK ALREADY!

THE CAR WON'T START. I THINK IT NEEDS GAS.

GAS!...YOU TOLD ME YOU FILLED THE TANK THIS MORNING!

I DID.

AT THE RISK OF BEING EXPOSED TO ONE OF YOUR ENDLESS SURPRISES...

HOW CAN IT BE OUT OF GAS IF YOU FILLED THE TANK THIS MORNING?

BECAUSE I HAVEN'T PUT IT BACK IN THE CAR YET..

71

72

HERMAN by JIM UNGER